For Kate and Harriet

Editor: Yves-Marie Maquet

Designer: Raymond Stoffel

Methuen/Moonlight
First published 1983 by Editions Gallimard
First published 1984 in Great Britain by Methuen
Children's Books Ltd, 11 New Fetter Lane, London EC4
in association with Moonlight Publishing Ltd,
131 Kensington Church Street, London W8
© 1983 by Editions Gallimard
English text and selection of poems © 1984
by Moonlight Publishing Ltd

Printed in Italy by La Editoriale Libraria

ISBN 0 907144 70 5

SHIPS AND SEAFARERS

DISCOVERERS

Text by Dominique Duviard
Translated and adapted by Sarah Matthews

Illustrations by Tony Ross

methuen ☽ moonlight

We are the boys to make her go –
With a doodah and a doodah!
Around Cape Horn in frost and snow –
Doodah, hoodah, day!
Blow, boys, blow,
For Californi-o!
There's plenty of gold,
so I've been told,
On the banks of Sacramento!

A shanty

The adventure of the sea

This sailor knows of wondrous lands afar,
More rich than Spain, when the Phoenicians shipped
Silver for common ballast ...
He told how isles sprang up and sank again,
Between short voyages, to his amaze;
And how the sea's sharp needles, firm and strong,
Ripped open the bellies of big, iron ships;
Of mighty icebergs in the Northern seas,
That haunt the far horizon like white ghosts ...

Oh, it was sweet
To hear that seaman tell such wondrous tales ...

W.H. Davies

The next few pages take you through the unfolding story of the sea. Use this chart to help you set the events in time as you read about them in the book.

What happened when?

The dawn of time: Noah's ark. Rafts. Hollowed tree-trunks as dugout canoes. Around **5000 BC**: the first Cretan ships.

Around **4000 BC** in Polynesia: canoes with outriggers and steerable rafts. Around **3500 BC**: wooden Egyptian barges on the Nile.

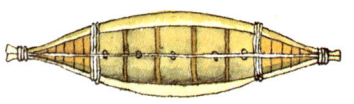

Around **2800 BC**: first maritime trade between the Phoenicians and the Egyptians. **2696 BC**: Cheops becomes Pharoah. The building of the great Pyramids, until about **2600 BC**.

Around **2000** to **1500 BC**: the Cretans and Phoenicians launch merchant ships and fighting ships in the Mediterranean.

Around **1490 BC**: Egyptian expedition to Punt. Around **1270 BC**, the defeat of Troy (and the start of Ulysses' wanderings).

Around **1250 BC**: Moses leads the Jews out of Egypt across the Red Sea. **1137 BC**: Nebuchadnezzar King of Babylon.

880 BC: the splendour of Nineveh and Jonah's close encounter with the whale: *'They took up Jonah, and cast him forth into the sea. The Lord had prepared a great fish to swallow up Jonah.*

Jonah was in the belly of the fish three days and three nights.'

Around **800 BC**, the Greek poet Homer writes the *Iliad* and the *Odyssey*.

10

480 BC: Salamis, the first naval battle in history.

Between **480** and **430 BC:** Life of Herodotus, the first real historian and geographer.

336 BC: beginning of the reign of Alexander the Great, King of Macedonia.

Between **350** and **330 BC:** expedition by the Greek Pytheas of Marseilles to the North Atlantic.

31 BC: the future Emperor Augustus defeats Anthony and Cleopatra's fleet at Actium in the Ionian Sea.

AD 440-50: Attila the Hun invades the West. Around **610:** Mahomet the Prophet and the beginnings of Islam. **649:** first Arab fleet in the Mediterranean.

Around **790:** the first Norman raids on England. **846** and **866:** the Normans besiege Paris.

871: Alfred the Great founds the Royal Navy. **983:** Eric the Red discovers Greenland.

1066: William the Conqueror crosses the Channel with a fleet of 1400 ships and beats the English at Hastings.

'King Harold met William at the grey apple tree. William came upon him unexpectedly. King Harold was slain there.' From a chronicle of the time.

1150-1300: the compass makes its appearance, is perfected and comes into general use in Western ships.

Between **1275** and **1295:** the travels of Marco Polo.

1339: beginning of the 100 Years' War between France and England.

Between **1396** and **1460:** Prince Henry of Portugal encourages voyages of exploration. The Portuguese discover the Azores, Senegal and the Cape Verd Islands.

1492: Christopher Columbus reaches the New World.

1497: Vasco da Gama travels from Lisbon to Calcutta by way of the Cape of Good Hope.

1509: Henry VIII becomes King of England.

1520: Magellan sails between Tierra del Fuego and the tip of South America to reach the Pacific Ocean.

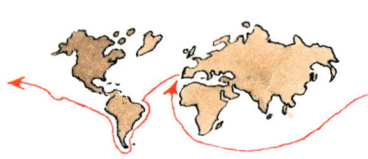

Meanwhile, Cortés and the Conquistadores carry Christianity, disease and gold-fever to Central America.

1571: led by the Venetians, the combined Christian fleets wipe out the Turkish fleet. It is the last major battle fought with galleys.

1588: the English rout the Armada of King Philip II of Spain. It is the first major naval encounter between sailing ships.

1603: Death of Queen Elizabeth I and accession of James I, leading to the union of the kingdoms of Scotland and England.

1608: the Dutch Netherlands win their independence from Spain. In the same year, Champlain, a Frenchman, founds Quebec in Canada.

1620: The *Mayflower* arrives in New England. **1626:** the founding of New Amsterdam, later to become New York. **1649:** the execution of Charles I.

1650-97: the golden age of piracy in the West Indies.
1688: the death of Morgan, 'the pirates' admiral'.

1660: the Restoration of the English monarchy. **1666:** the Great Fire of London.

1698: attempted English colony at Darien in Central America ousted by the Spanish. **1705:** the sailor Alexander Selkirk is shipwrecked, alone, on the Island of Juan Fernandez. His experiences inspire Defoe's *Robinson Crusoe*.

1759: storming of the Heights of Abraham, and Wolfe's victory, and death, at Quebec.

From **1766** to **1779,** Bougainville and Cook explore the Pacific.

1776: the American Declaration of Independence.

1787: the mutiny on the *Bounty*.

The Admiralty sends the frigate *Pandora* to hunt down the mutineers. Those who are caught are court-martialled.

1789: the French Revolution.
1795-1825: the exploits of French corsairs during the Revolutionary and Napoleonic Wars make them national heroes.

1797-8: Coleridge composes *The Rime of the Ancient Mariner*.

May 1803: England declares war on France. **1805:** the Battle of Trafalgar.

1815: Waterloo and the end of Napoleon's empire. **1816:** the first steam crossing of the Channel. The *Elise* later navigates up the Seine as far as Paris.

1815: the Treaty of Vienna outlaws the black slave trade. The end, in theory, of the 'black triangle'. In theory, not in fact.

1833-4: Britain abolishes slavery.
1843: Edgar Allen Poe publishes *The Golden Scarab*, the tale of Captain Kidd. Pirates have become storybook heroes.

1851: the schooner *America* wins the cup which, for over 130 years, will continue to carry her name.

1854-6: the Crimean War. Florence Nightingale helps wounded soldiers and founds the nursing profession.

1857: the English launch the biggest ship yet built, the *Great Eastern*, powered by steam to travel up to a speed of 14.5 knots.

1861: Herman Melville publishes *Moby Dick*.

1861-5: The American Civil War ends by maintaining the Union and liberating the slaves.

1882: Stevenson publishes *Treasure Island*

1892: construction of the *Fram*, in wood, to the plans of architect Colin Archer. Nansen uses this ship on all his Arctic explorations.

1901: death of Queen Victoria.

The American Peary reaches the North Pole on **6th April 1909.**

1911: the Norwegian Amundsen reaches the South Pole just over a month before Captain Scott.

1914: Shackleton's *Endurance* is ice-bound in the Wedell Sea. The crew abandon ship. The vessel is crushed to pieces 10 months later.

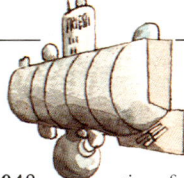

1948: construction of Auguste Piccard's bathscaphe *Trieste*.

1950: Cousteau launches his research ship, *Calypso*, and puts the finishing touches to the aqualung he has invented in association with Emile Gagnan.

1952: launching of the *Nautilus*, the first nuclear-propelled submarine (US Navy).

1983: *Australia II*, skippered by John Bertrand, beats *Liberty*, skippered by Dennis Conner, to win the America's Cup.

15

Mythical mariners

The Sirens were mythical forerunners of the mermaid but, instead of a woman's body and a fish's tail, they had a bird's body and a woman's head.

After the end of the Trojan War, **Ulysses** tried to get back to his island home. Unfortunately, some of the Gods on Olympus had other ideas and set traps for him. He had to pass the Sirens, who lured sailors to their deaths by singing so sweetly they leaped towards them into the sea, and drowned. Ulysses, though, forewarned by the sorceress Circe, had his rowers plug their ears with wax so that they could not hear the Sirens' song. Firmly tied to the mast so that he would not jump overboard, he was the only man to hear the Sirens' song and live.

The adventures of Ulysses are told by the Greek poet Homer in two books, the *Iliad* and the *Odyssey*.

A wonderful bird called a Roc.

Scholars have spent long hours trying to pin down just where in the Mediterranean Ulysses' adventures might have taken place. There is, for instance, a mountain in Italy called Circeo, which could be where he spent some time with the sorceress Circe.

Sinbad the sailor was the hero of Arab stories in the Middle Ages. The tales of his seven journeys are told by Scheherazade in the *Thousand and One Nights*. His adventures were like those of Ulysses: storms, shipwreck, fights with a man-eating giant, a huge snake and all sorts of other awful creatures.

The Roc was a gigantic bird with legs 'as large as the trunk of a tree'. It carried Sinbad into the air 'up and up till he could no longer see the earth'.

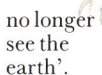

The Egyptians and the Phoenicians

The Egyptians were not really very good navigators, but they were good at boat-building. They started by building boats to carry goods on the Nile. Gradually they travelled farther and farther down the river and along the coastline. Queen Hatshepsut sent an expedition to a country called Punt (probably present-day Somalia) to trade in incense and myrrh. The Egyptians set up a number of important expeditions, although they did not take part in them themselves.

In 1969 Thor Heyerdahl built and sailed this replica of an Egyptian papyrus boat.

The historian Herodotus tells how, on one trip, the pharaoh sent a fleet manned by Phoenicians into the Red Sea. He told them to come back by way of the Mediterranean and the Straits of Gibraltar. They took three years to do it, having reached the edge of the Indian Ocean and the South Atlantic. When they got back, they told how, on the farthest part of their voyage, they had seen the sun in the north instead of the south. To us that means that they had crossed the Equator into the southern hemisphere. At the time it was just set down as a typical traveller's tall story.

This is one of the boats in use at the time of the expedition to Punt (about 1500 BC). It is about 28 metres long and has a rope tied from keel to stern to stop the ends of the boat, which aren't supported by the water, from collapsing.

19

Beyond the Mediterranean...

Pytheas was a Greek astronomer. He lived in the Phocean colony of present-day Marseilles, in the south of France.

In the fourth century BC you had to be very wise or very brave to venture beyond the limits of the known world, and out of the Mediterranean.

Even on the Mediterranean, sailors could only navigate by sight, and would try to find a beach or to anchor their ships at night Crossings were rare, and followed well-defined routes dictated by prevailing winds. They could not sail against the wind. So you had either to be very wise or very brave! Pytheas was both.

Marseilles was a wealthy trading city, with merchants prepared to pay for an expedition travelling beyond the Mediterranean. They had already seen the Phoenicians of Carthage coming back from such voyages with important goods such as tin. Tin, mixed with copper, formed the bronze needed to make weapons.

First of all, Pytheas went to Gades (Cadiz), where he prepared for his voyage. Then he set off for the north, sailing along the coastline of what would later be known as Spain, Portugal and France. He reached Cornwall in England, and, navigating up the coast of England, got as far as Scotland.

...where the sun never sets in summer

Finally, 'six days' sailing from there', he discovered a land that he called Thule, 'where the sun never sets in summer'. This might have been one of the Shetland Islands, or the Orkneys, or even the north of Norway. The story of what he found on his journey was published, but has since been lost. Ironically, all that we know about Pytheas comes from historians of the time who did not believe a word he said, and quoted him only to make fun of him. They were the ones who were wrong, though. Pytheas was an outstanding astronomer. He could calculate latitude from the angle of the sun to the horizon, and all the distances that he gave seem about right.

Pytheas' boat must have been like this one: two oars for steering with; square sails to take advantage of the prevailing winds; and a bank of oars on each side to be used if there was no wind.

The first ships were built to serve as both warships and transport ships. Slowly their construction changed. They were able to travel farther and farther and at the same time, two different kinds of ship developed. There were heavy, wide boats that were used for transport, and narrow, faster boats with a beak that could be used for ramming – these were the fighting ships. In the picture below, you can see the two banks of big oars used to propel this sort of galley, or *bireme*.

The first known naval battle took place in **480 BC** near the island of Salamis opposite Athens in Greece. The combined Greek forces were fighting off a Persian invasion led by King Xerxes. The Greek fleet was much smaller than the Persians', but the Athenian commander, Themistocles, lured the Persians into a very narrow stretch of water between the island and the mainland.

The Persians could squeeze only a small number of their ships into the front line. Making use of the local winds, Themistocles drove a wedge of ships through the Persian lines. Xerxes' ships were so closely packed that they pushed up against each other, breaking their banks of oars. The battle went on from dawn to dusk, but by the end of the day the Greeks were masters of the sea.

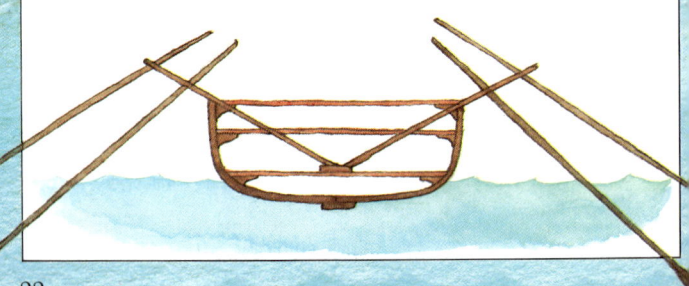

First sea battles

At the bottom of the page, you can see a Roman sea-fight. The ship on the left is just putting out a *corvus*, a boarding-bridge which dropped over the prow and clamped onto the enemy ship with grappling irons. (It was called a *corvus*, which means 'crow' in Latin, because the long bridge sticking forward in the ship looked like a crow's beak.) Soldiers are standing ready on the bridge to drop into the ship on the right and fight the enemy hand to hand.

The *corvus* was a good fighting weapon, but it had its disadvantages. It made the galleys dangerously top-heavy. After almost their entire fleet had been blown over and sunk in a storm, the Romans decided that lighter naval weapons might be a good idea.

The Vikings

A furore Normannorum libera nos, domine! (From the fury of the Norsemen, good Lord, deliver us!) This was the prayer that went up in English Churches when a Viking raid threatened. For over 200 years, **from AD 789 onwards,** Europe lay in fear of these fierce raiders. In ones or twos, or in great fleets, the Vikings pushed out from Scandinavia, looking for land and loot. Following the coastlines and making use of currents, they first raided, and then settled, in the British Isles, France and Italy. They rowed up the great rivers into the heart of Russia. Viking communities were set up in Iceland and Greenland. They even made their way to North America.

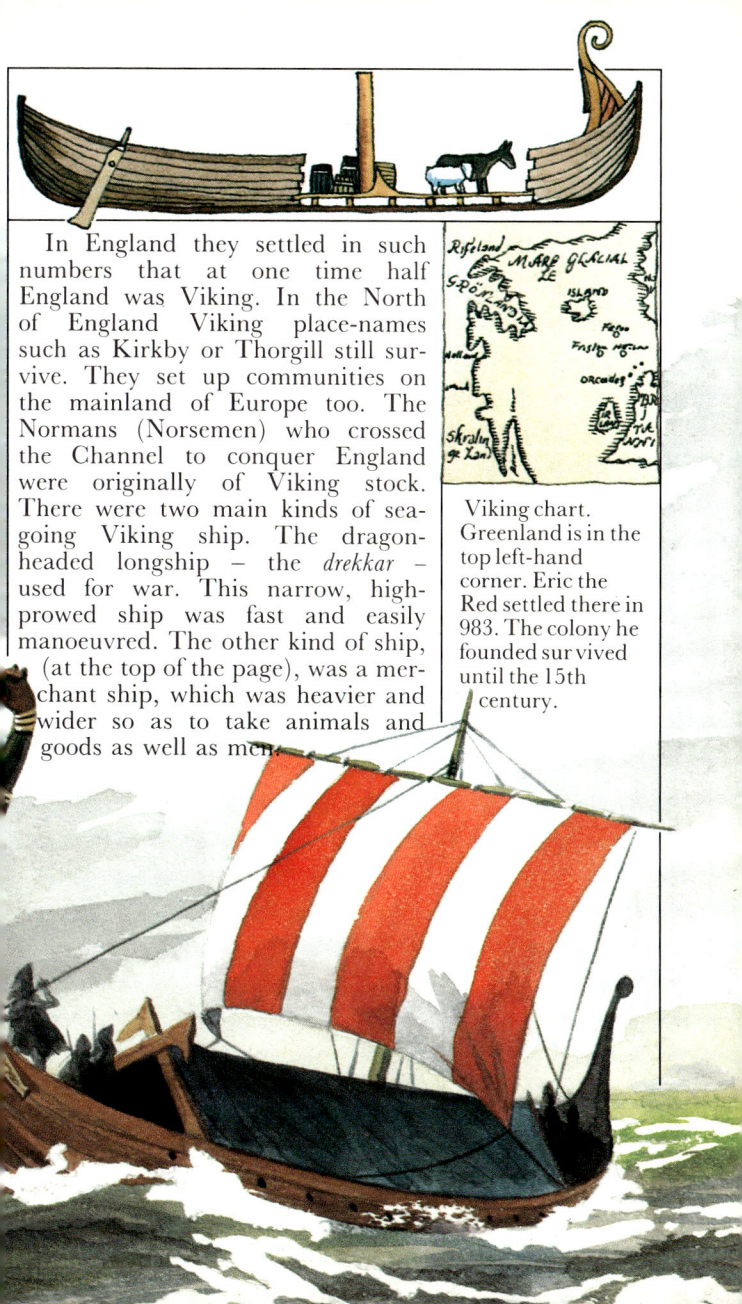

In England they settled in such numbers that at one time half England was Viking. In the North of England Viking place-names such as Kirkby or Thorgill still survive. They set up communities on the mainland of Europe too. The Normans (Norsemen) who crossed the Channel to conquer England were originally of Viking stock. There were two main kinds of seagoing Viking ship. The dragon-headed longship – the *drekkar* – used for war. This narrow, high-prowed ship was fast and easily manoeuvred. The other kind of ship, (at the top of the page), was a merchant ship, which was heavier and wider so as to take animals and goods as well as men.

Viking chart. Greenland is in the top left-hand corner. Eric the Red settled there in 983. The colony he founded survived until the 15th century.

Christopher Columbus

12 October 1492: Columbus discovers the New World by mistake. He was looking for India and Japan. At the time he set sail the Earth was thought to be about a third smaller than it is, and Asia was supposed to stretch much farther east. So Columbus thought that a fairly short voyage westwards from the Atlantic islands would take him to the Spice Islands of the East Indies. There was a lot of money to be made trading in spices.

Columbus was not alone in thinking that India could be reached by travelling westwards, but testing the theory was expensive. Eventually Queen Isabella of Spain paid for the expedition.

These islands are the most fertile, and temperate and flat and good in the whole world. Christopher Columbus

Queen Isabella paid for three ships, the *Nina*, the *Pinta*, and the *Santa Maria* to be fitted out. Setting off in August 1492 from Cadiz in Spain with 120 men, Columbus reached the Bahamas three months later. He named the island where he landed San Salvador. He was convinced that the islands he had found were just off the mainland of India. He called them the West Indies, and the inhabitants Indians. Because of Columbus' original mistake, the peoples of the American continent have been called Indians ever since.

Christopher Columbus made four other voyages between 1493 and 1502, exploring Dominica, Guadaloupe, Jamaica, Trinidad, and the coasts of Venezuela, the Honduras, Nicaragua and Panama.

Magellan

Magellan was Portuguese, brought up as a page at the Portuguese court. But when he was 37 he quarrelled with the King of Portugal and moved to Spain. It was the Spanish king who paid for his expedition.

The world was round. Scholars had known that in theory since ancient times, but it still had not been proved.

It was known that there was an ocean on the other side of America. Balboa had crossed Central America and found it in 1513.

How to get by boat from one ocean to the other? That was the problem. It was the expedition led by Magellan which solved it in **1520.**

Knowing that no gap had been found in the American coastline, Magellan decided to find where the continent ended. With five ships and 270 men he set sail southwards. It was a terrible journey. One ship was lost, another mutinied and turned back. Eventually, though, he found the straits which are named after him. The expedition took five weeks to battle out of the Atlantic Ocean and through the straits against the prevailing wind, past rocks and barren land. Then they found the other ocean, stretching before them in perfect calm. Magellan called it the peaceful, or Pacific Ocean.

Once in the Pacific Ocean, Magellan calculated that he must be very close to the Spice Islands, and set out to find them. In fact, the expedition sailed for 98 days before seeing land. On the journey the ships ran out of provisions. The crews ate leather and sawdust. Boiled rats were a treat. At last they reached the Philippines. They had linked the westward and eastward routes.

Magellan never reached home again. He was killed by Philippine islanders.

Of all those who had set out, one ship, the *Victoria*, and 19 survivors finally got back to Spain. They were the first men to sail right round the world.

You can see from this picture of the *Victoria* how small she was.

These men are Spanish soldiers. When they first arrived in Mexico, their general, Cortés, ordered that the boats they came in should be burnt. That way they could not run away, they had to stay and fight. Now they have become *conquistadores*, conquerors, and are building a boat to take them, and the gold they have plundered, home.

Using local wood to build their boat, they have become the first shipyard workers in America . . .

The Conquistadores

This is Hernando Cortés accepting the surrender of the Aztec emperor.

He looks pleasant enough here, but he was a determined and ruthless general. He arrived in Mexico with a tiny army (400 men, 15 horses, 13 muskets and 7 small cannon) and conquered the Aztec empire. It was partly luck – many of the Aztecs greeted the Spaniards as gods come back to create a Heaven on Earth. They soon found out their mistake. Cortés knew he could not beat the Aztecs by force of arms, so he used terror, torture and treachery to win the day. The Emperor Montezuma, inviting the Spaniards into his palace as honoured guests, soon found himself held prisoner, forced to issue their orders in his own name. When his people attacked the palace to rescue him, Montezuma was killed in the fighting.

In just over 20 years, from the discovery of the Pacific coast by Balboa in **1513** to the conquest of the Inca Empire in Peru by Pizarro in **1535,** the Spanish carved out an empire in the Americas, 'for God and the king' – and for gold . . .

The first Aztecs to be baptized.

The Aztecs seize the palace where their emperor is a prisoner.

The Spanish and the Aztecs fighting on the lake surrounding the city. These illustrations are based on Aztec miniatures.

The invincible Armada

Francis Drake

In 1588 King Philip II of Spain decided to invade England with a fleet of 130 ships and an army of over 8000 soldiers. This armed fleet, or 'Armada', was so impressive the Spanish called it 'invincible'.

Under their admiral, Francis Drake, the English pursued the Spanish fleet as it sailed up the Channel. But, although there was a great deal of gunfire, nobody seemed to be winning.

> *I sent my fleet to fight the English, not the elements.*
>
> Philip II

The Spanish fleet came to rest outside Calais, where it was supposed to collect the invasion army. But the army could not get out to the galleons, because their barges were shot out of the water the moment they left harbour. At the same time, the galleons could not go and fetch the army, because the water in the harbour was too shallow for them. While the Spanish dithered, Drake struck, sending fireships filled with burning straw and gunpowder in among the enemy galleons. The Spanish panicked and fled. What the English had begun, the weather finished, driving the scattered Spanish fleet before it onto the craggy coasts of Scotland and Ireland. Only 63 ships returned to Spain. The rest were lost.

The New World

New York

The bay of New York was discovered by an Italian, Giovanni da Verrazzano, in 1524.

Nearly a 100 years later the Dutch settled on the island of Manhattan, buying it from the local Indians for the equivalent of 25 dollars. They called their settlement New Amsterdam.

In 1644 the leaders of the community invited the British to come and save them from their domineering governor, Peter Stuyvesant. The British rechristened the town New York.

The *Mayflower* ties up and the first of the Pilgrim Fathers step ashore.

Boston

On 6 September 1620 a small English ship, the *Mayflower*, set out for America. She had nearly 100 people on board. Among them were 36 Puritans. They were going to the New World to find more freedom to follow their beliefs and customs than the English government would allow them at home. The *Mayflower*'s journey took two and half months. When they reached land, nearly 200 miles farther north than they had expected, the Pilgrim Fathers, as the Puritans called themselves, founded a colony at New Plymouth near Boston in Massachusetts. There they drew up the *Mayflower Compact*, the first American constitution. The Pilgrim Fathers were the founders of what was to become the United States of America.

This picture shows what Boston looked like to an artist at the time.

Almost 20 years before the Pilgrim Fathers, Sir Walter Raleigh had pioneered the way and sent expeditions to this part of the New World.

Galleons

On **24 August 1724** a cyclone struck the *Conde de Tolosa*, a Spanish ship carrying cargo to the New World. The ship was driven onto the coral reefs off the island of Hispaniola (now Santa Dominica). A hole was gashed in the hull and the ship went down, leaving only the tip of the mast sticking up above water level. Eight of the crew managed to haul themselves up onto what had been the crow's nest, now a life-saving platform clear of the rocks and the patrolling sharks. It was over a month before the seven who survived were saved.

An 18th-century Spanish galleon.

*Stately Spanish galleon coming from the Isthmus,
Dipping through the tropics by the palm-green shores,
With a cargo of diamonds,
Emeralds, amethysts,
Topazes, and cinnamon, and gold moidores.*

John Masefield

After the discovery of the New World, huge transatlantic fleets were created **in the 16th century** to carry the riches plundered from the Americas back to Europe.

The heavy Spanish ships had to make their way through dangerous waters, where shipwrecks were frequent. Not only that, but they were attacked by the pirates who infested the Bahama islands.

Much of the gold looted from the Incas and the Aztecs still lies at the bottom of the Caribbean, waiting to be found by divers searching for sunken treasure.

Corsairs and pirates

1773 — 1827
Robert Surcouf and his pistols.

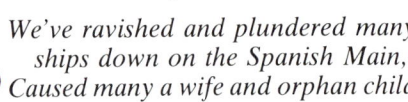

Surcouf, the French privateer, raided English ships. Two famous English pirates were Blackbeard and Captain Kidd. Both ended their days dangling from a hangman's noose.

My name is Edward Hallahan, as you may understand,
I was born in Waterford in Ireland's happy land.
My parents raised me tenderly in the care of God likewise,
But little did I think I'd die 'neath Cuba's sunny skies . . .

We've ravished and plundered many ships down on the Spanish Main,
Caused many a wife and orphan child in sorrow to complain.
We caused their crew to walk the plank, gave them a watery grave,
The saying of our captain was, 'A dead man tells no tales'.

A ballad

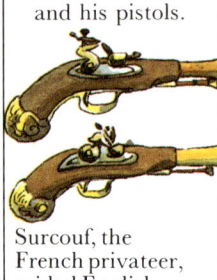

Corsairs, pirates, privateers . . . What is the difference between them? Let's take the nastiest ones, the pirates, first. They have always existed everywhere. Lawless, faithless, greedy and cruel, they are the thugs and muggers of the seaways. Their flags were designed to frighten, and they still do . . .

Corsairs and privateers behaved like pirates, but legally. Given *letters of commission* by their sovereigns, they became captains in the royal service. Their mission was to attack the enemy's merchant ships. Since they were paid a percentage of anything they looted, they carried out their orders enthusiastically.

Blackbeard

Christopher Condent

'Calico Jack' Rackam

Bartholomew Roberts

A Barbadian Head
A Martinican Head

The *Wasa* and the *Mary Rose*

The *Mary Rose* and the *Wasa* were raised by being pumped full of air and hauled to the surface with ropes.

In 1628, in Stockholm, the finest ship of the 17th century was under construction. She was called the *Wasa* after the Swedish royal family. She was 70 metres long, 12 metres wide, and carried 64 bronze cannon. Hundreds of carpenters had been working on her for over two years.

Finally, the day that she was to be launched arrived. Fully rigged, she slid into the water. Her sails bellying in the wind, her gunports open to show off her gleaming new cannon. Slowly she started to turn around in the harbour in order to come back to the quayside.

Oh my gentlemen, oh my gallant men!

Henry VIII as he saw the *Mary Rose* go down.

Suddenly a gust of wind caught her. She heeled over and water began pouring into her open gunports. Within three minutes the pride of the Swedish navy lay 35 metres deep at the bottom of Stockholm harbour.

The *Mary Rose* had gone down in 1545 in almost the same way. Sailing out to meet the French fleet, with the vice-admiral of the English forces on board, she was laden with guns and ammunition. Her gunports were open, ready to fire. As she turned into the wind, the water flooded in and she sank in minutes. Of about 500 on board, some 25 were saved. The rest, said someone who saw it happen, were 'drowned like rats'.

The sea and the mud preserved these two ships almost intact for over 300 years. The *Wasa* was raised in 1961 and the *Mary Rose* in 1982. Both ships provide a wealth of information about sailing and sailors of the time.

Galleys

Shackles

Galleys were used as warships until **the end of the 16th century.** They were still used for transport and other naval support duties for nearly another 200 years.

Although they had sails, they were mainly powered by banks of huge oars along both sides. Pulling the oars was hard work. At first slaves or enemy captives were used as oarsmen. Later, condemned criminals were sentenced to serve time 'at the oar'. They had a very rough life.

This picture shows a French galley of the type used until 1720. The oars were each 12 metres long.

*The salt made the oar-handles
like shark-skin;
our knees were cut to the
bone with salt-cracks;
our hair was stuck to our
foreheads;
and our lips were cut to
the gums,
and you whipped us because
we could not row.*

Will you never let us go?

Rudyard Kipling

The slavers

Many merchants and planters came on board. They put us in groups and examined us attentively. They also made us jump . . . We thought . . . we should be eaten by these ugly men, as they appeared to us; and, when soon after we were all put down under the deck again, there was much dread and trembling.

From *The Interesting Narrative of the Life of Olaudah Equiano . . . the African. Written by himself.* 1791.

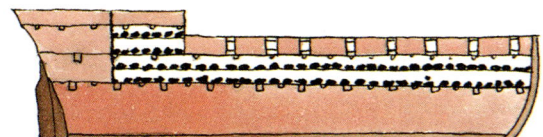

The colonies in America and the West Indies had much fertile land, where settlers established plantations, growing crops to be sold in Europe. But, though they had the land, they did not have enough people to work it. So they bought slaves from Africa.

The traders bringing the slaves from Africa worked out a system to make the most money possible from their trips. Setting off from Europe, they loaded their ships with arms and other goods. When they arrived in Africa, they exchanged their cargoes for slaves provided by Arab raiders or by rival African tribes. From there they sailed to America, and again changed cargoes, swapping the slaves for sugar, cotton and tobacco . . .

The slave trade was abolished by the Treaty of Vienna in 1815. Slavery itself was made illegal in England and her colonies and territories in 1833-4.

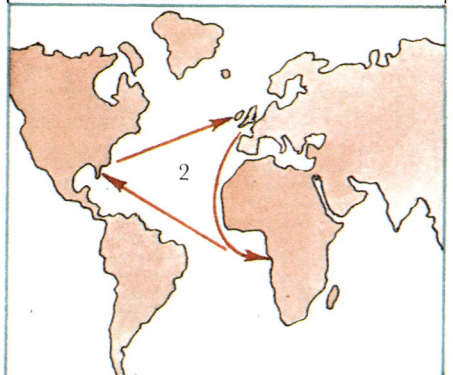

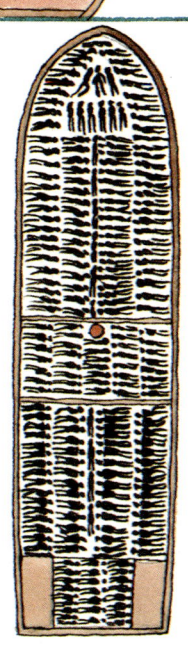

1. This shows how the slaves were packed in, shackled, below decks. Conditions were so bad that over half the 'cargo' would die on the voyage.

2. The 'black triangle'.

The age of scientific exploration

Cook: *It has always been a principle with me to punish the least offence committed by my men against these primitive peoples: that they should steal from us is no reason for us to do the same to them.*

Cook discovers Easter Island with its huge stone statues.

Terra australis incognita ... An unknown land in the south.

Ever since it had been proved that the world was round, scientists had supposed that there must be a vast continent in the southern hemisphere to counterbalance all the land in the North. Otherwise, they thought, the world would tip over ...

So, **in the 18th century,** two great explorers, Bougainville, a Frenchman, and an Englishman, James Cook, set off separately to find this continent.

During his voyage Bougainville discovered the Polynesian islands, while Cook on his three trips, between 1768 and 1780, found the scattered islands of Melanesia, New Zealand and finally, Australia – the Land in the South. All these lands together, though, including Antarctica, did not add up to the vast continent expected. That was proved a fable once and for all.

In 1788 the first Governor of Australia set up his headquarters at Port Jackson, calling it 'the finest harbour in the world'. Port Jackson is now Sydney.

Bougainville set off on his journey in 1766, and reached Tahiti two years later. After their long voyage, the crew thought they were in heaven. As the Frenchmen approached the shore, the native Tahitians pushed off from the beach in hundreds of canoes and surrounded them, smiling at them, embracing them, giving them presents.

When they returned home, Bougainville persuaded a young Tahitian chief called Aotooroo to go back with them. He wanted to show Parisian society the goodness and honesty of a man uncorrupted by Western 'civilization'.

Unfortunately Aotooroo soon became homesick and ill. After a short stay in Paris, Bougainville arranged to take him back to Tahiti. He died on the voyage.

Louis-Antoine de Bougainville.

They found such a profusion of plants in that bay...

Cook's three voyages took him even farther than Bougainville. Crisscrossing the Pacific Ocean, he charted important parts of the New Zealand and Australian coastlines, as well as discovering most of the islands of any size scattered across the Pacific.

Cook was a fair captain, and his crews were devoted to him. He was very interested in using the latest scientific discoveries, not only for his explorations, but also to improve the conditions and safety of his crews. He took powdered soup and pickled vegetables with him to keep his men healthy on the long voyages. He was the first man to use the new 'chronometer', which made navigation much more precise and, consequently, safer.

Naturalists' sketches brought back by Cook and Bougainville.

. . . that I called it Botany Bay.
Captain Cook

Both Cook and Bougainville took various scientists with them on their voyages. There were map-makers, geographers, naturalists, botanists, even painters, such as William Hodges, who brought back splendid pictures of the newly discovered lands. Sketches made by Parkinson (on Cook's voyages) and Commerson (on Bougainville's) were important in helping to identify all the new plants and animals. There were, after all, no photographs then.

Cook never came back from his third voyage. He was clubbed to death in a surprise attack by Hawaian islanders. Crew members who escaped from the attack and made it back to the ship climbed aboard in tears, crying: 'We have lost our father! Our father is gone!'

The inhabitants of New Zealand are as modest and reserved in their behaviour and conversation as the most polite nations of Europe. Both sexes mark their bodies with black stains. The paintings resemble filigree work, and the foliage in old ornaments.

Captain Cook

The *Bounty*

The big nations of Europe had shared out the world between them. Each had its own colonies. These colonies could not have survived without sailors and their ships to bring them supplies and to take their produce away to sell.

Yet sailors had a hard life on board ship. They could be severely punished for breaches of discipline.

The famous ill-fated journey of the

Bounty shows what could happen when things went wrong.

The *Bounty* set out **in 1787,** under the command of Captain Bligh, to fetch plants back from Tahiti. The voyage was very long and difficult, and Tahiti was so delightful by comparison that the crew could hardly face the journey home. They set off, but Bligh's severe treatment finally snapped the little patience the sailors had left. They mutinied. A few of the crew stayed loyal to the captain. They were set adrift with Captain Bligh, and very few provisions, in one of the ship's longboats. It was only Bligh's single-mindedness which brought them safely across the sea to an island near Java, a journey of nearly 5000 kilometres.

The mutineers finally settled on Pitcairn, a small rocky island miles from anywhere in the middle of the Pacific. Their descendants live there still.

Brutal punishments were common in the Navy. As well as flogging with the 'cat-o'-nine-tails' (a lead-tipped whip) there was *keel-hauling* for serious offences. Condemned men were tied to a rope and pulled round the ship from one side to the other under water. They often drowned, or died of the wounds inflicted by the sharp barnacles which tore the skin off them as they were dragged across the ship's bottom.

1. *Traverse-board:* for marking the distance and direction of a course covered over a period of time (16th century).
2. *Quadrant* (15th century).
3. *Astrolabe* (15th century). This and the quadrant made it possible for sailors to take the altitudes of stars.
4. *Nocturnal:* for measuring the time of night by calculating the angle of the Pole Star (16th century).
5. *Hour-glass:* for measuring time.
6-7. *Davis quadrants* (16th and 17th centuries).
8. *Arbaletus* (15th and 16th centuries).
9. *Octant* (18th century). These four instruments were improvements on the early astrolabes and quadrants.

Some of the instruments used through the ages to help sailors navigate. Many of them can be seen today in the National Maritime Museum at Greenwich near London.

The art of navigation

How can you find out where you are when you're out of sight of land, bobbing up and down on the sea? The only things that you can see which don't change with the wind and tide are the sun and the stars, and they're what sailors steer by.

The Egyptians and Phoenicians navigated by the stars. But it was not until the 15th century that European navigation became really scientific, with the development of the compass and sea charts.

In the 18th century the *log-line* was used as a way of measuring speed and distance. Knots were tied in a cable at regular intervals, then the cable was let out, over a set period of time, to trail in the water behind the ship. When the time was up, the cable was hauled in, and the number of knots that had been let out showed how fast the ship was going.

That is why the speed of craft travelling on water is measured in 'knots' to this day. 1 knot is the equivalent of about 1.9 kilometres an hour.

Trafalgar

Nelson's 'stroke of genius': two columns (A and B) cut the enemy line and attacked each segment separately.

England expects that every man will do his duty

Nelson's last signal.

May the great God, whom I worship, grant to my country, and for the benefit of Europe in general, a great and glorious victory; and may no misconduct in anyone tarnish it; and may humanity after victory be the predominant feature in the British fleet.

So wrote Nelson just before the Battle of Trafalgar.

Napoleon, the French Emperor, had already conquered most of Europe when he decided that his Empire would not be safe unless he conquered England too.

But England could only be reached by sea. So it was important to be master of the sea. However, though Napoleon knew all about fighting on land, the English had a genius at fighting at sea: Horatio Nelson.

Nelson met the French fleet at Trafalgar, just outside Cadiz, on **21 October 1805.** His strategy of sailing straight at the enemy line in two columns was dangerous but decisive. The English won a crushing victory, with almost half the enemy fleet captured or sunk.

Nelson himself was killed at Trafalgar. The French Admiral, Villeneuve, also died as a result of the battle. Defeated and in disgrace, he went back to France and killed himself.

The clippers

As sea travel became easier and safer, world trade developed and, with it, competition.

If merchants in London were waiting for tea to sell to their customers, the first ship to arrive with the tea could ask the highest price. So ships became faster and faster, racing each other across the world's oceans. Some, the sleekest and fastest, were called 'clippers' because of the way they 'clipped' along.

On **30 May 1866** the *Taeping*, the *Ariel* and the *Serica*, three English tea-clippers, set out from China in a race for England.

The *Taeping* reached the London Docks at a quarter to nine in the evening of 6 September.

The *Ariel* arrived at a quarter past nine, and the *Serica* at a quarter to eleven.

260,000 kilometres and a three months' voyage, and only two hours separating first and last . . .

Ships such as these were often also heavily laden with wool from Australia, minerals from South America, wheat from North America and coal from Europe. Nearly all of them had to navigate the terrible seas around Cape Horn.

The opening of the Suez Canal in 1869 meant that the bigger cargo steamers could compete in speed with the clippers, and carry more cargo. The age of sail was over.

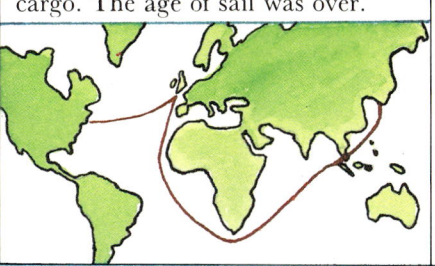

A map of some of the trade routes.

Exploring the Poles

William Barents (1550-95), a Dutchman, was an early Polar explorer. Trying to find a north-east passage from Europe to Asia, he discovered the islands of Novaya Zemlaya, to the north of Russia. Barents died of cold while exploring the sea which still bears his name.

At the beginning of the 20th century there were still two big blank areas on maps of the world: the North Pole and the South Pole.

Peary, an American, was the first to reach the North Pole in 1909. In 1911, the Norwegian Amundsen and Captain Scott, an Englishman, raced for the honour of reaching the South Pole first. Amundsen planted the Norwegian flag there just 27 days before Scott arrived. Scott and his party died on the return journey. Although many of the ships used by these explorers were lost, some can still be seen today. Shackleton's *Endurance* was crushed in the ice of the Weddell Sea in 1914.

Nansen's *Fram* wintering in the ice.

*And ice, mast-high, came floating by,
As green as emerald.*

S.T. Coleridge

But the *Fram*, Nansen's ship, and the *Discovery*, which carried Scott's ill-fated expedition, still survive. You can see the *Fram* in a special museum in Oslo, while the *Discovery* is moored on the Thames in London.

Shackleton and his ship, the *Endurance*.

Ships from Europe, sailing over the Seven Seas from the 15th century onwards, found that there were other civilizations with their own different but highly developed and efficient boats.

Chinese junks and Arab dhows

The Chinese have long been skilful seamen, navigating the great rivers of China and the China sea. They invented the earliest compass. The two main types of Chinese boat, the junk and the sampan, are very similar. Sampans (1) are smaller, carrying goods on rivers and in coastal areas, while junks (2) can sail in the open sea. They have flat bottoms, and their sails have bamboo battens across them, making them easy to fold up or open out. They can also be rowed with a big oar over the stern, which is moved from side to side like a fish's tail.

The Arabs too were great sailors. The dhow (3), with its keel made of planks sewn edge to edge, and its big sails, made it possible for them to sail long distances in the open sea.

Boats like these were developed in the 11th century and are still used by the Chinese and Arabs today.

From sail...

1. The *Archduke Ludovic* was the first steamship of the Lloyd Triestino line, sailing to the Middle East (1837).

Paddle-wheel

Archimedes screw.

2. The *Castor* was one of the first French steamships (1830).
3. The *Willapa*. A motorized Finnish schooner, specially adapted for carrying wood.
4. The *Rattler* demonstrated the superiority of the Archimedes screw over the paddle-wheel by defeating its twin ship, the *Alecto*, in a tug-o'-war in 1845.

. . . to steam

5. The American steamship *Thomas Anderson*.

Below, the *Normandie* (1937) was the first electrically propelled liner. Her boilers turned a generator which fed current to four electric motors.

The *Normandie* won the Atlantic Blue Riband for a crossing which reached speeds of over 30 knots. The *Queen Elizabeth II*, below, was the last great liner in regular service on the North Atlantic crossing.

Triple screw.

The *Savannah*, below, was the first nuclear powered merchant ship. She can travel 336,000 miles without refuelling. Speed: 20.5 knots.

The hovercraft, a British invention, travels on a cushion of air.

The liners

As steam-power was developed, cargo and passenger liners began to ply the oceans of the world. The most important route of all was across the North Atlantic, between Europe and America.

Conditions at first were fairly rugged. Rats were known to gnaw at the cargo, and even to eat the corks out of the passengers' champagne bottles, until a regulation was established. No ship could leave Southampton until the captain had made sure that he had at least two cats on board.

Gradually passenger liners became more and more luxurious: with ballrooms, chandeliers, swimming pools, and sumptuous cabins, each with its own bathroom.

Before the age of the jet-plane, the speed with which liners could cross the Atlantic was all-important in the contest for passengers. Ships raced each other back and forth as fast as they could go. In 1935 the French liner *Normandie* broke all records for a transatlantic crossing. She went so fast that the paint was stripped off her hull.

You can see, below, how vast she was in comparison with earlier ships. She was 313 metres long. The *Normandie* was destroyed by fire in New York harbour in 1942.

The last of the great Atlantic liners, the British ship, *Queen Elizabeth II* – the third and final Cunard 'Queen' – was launched in 1968.

On 15 April 1912, during her maiden voyage, the 'unsinkable' liner *Titanic* hit an iceberg and went down. The ship's orchestra played popular songs for over two hours to prevent panic among the passengers. The entire orchestra, along with some 1600 others, was drowned. Of all on board, only 705 were saved.

65

Merchant ships

Container ships are the fastest merchant ships. They can often travel at over 25 knots.

Modern petrol tankers are huge. They are so big that the crews sometimes use bicycles to get from one end of the deck to the other. Because they are so enormous, petrol tankers are very fragile. The model boats you see sailing in your local pond are much stronger in comparison. When you put a model boat 'in dry dock', you rest it on two supports, one at each end. If you did that with a petrol tanker, it would snap in two!

This petrol tanker is discharging its cargo. Crude oil is being pumped along a pipeline to the terminal.

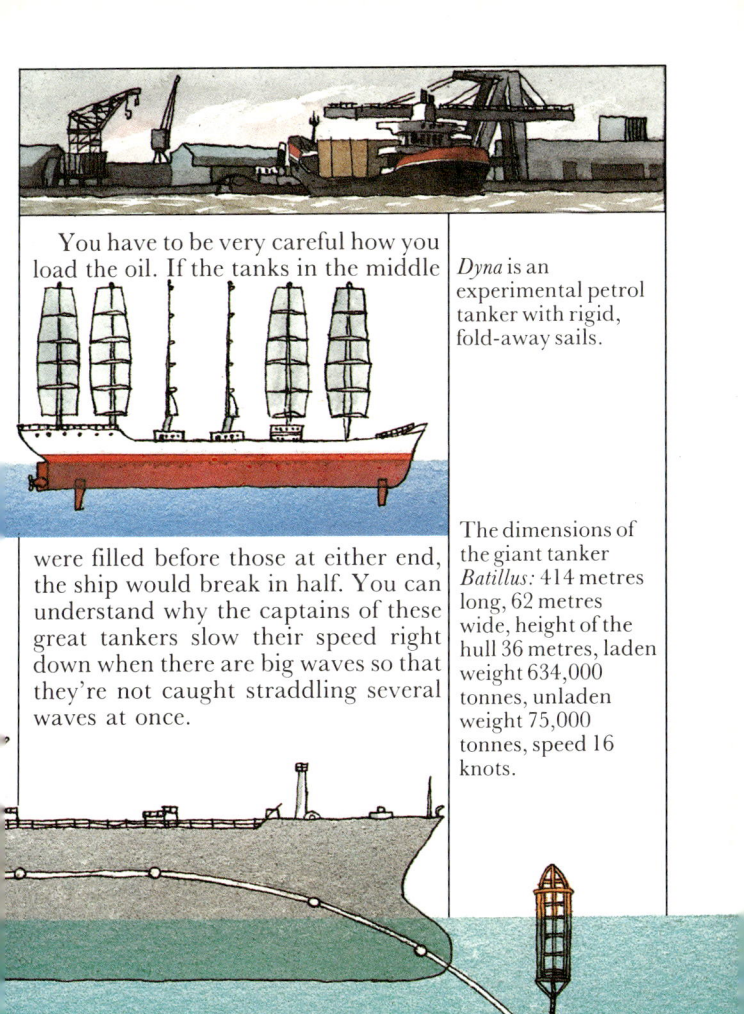

You have to be very careful how you load the oil. If the tanks in the middle were filled before those at either end, the ship would break in half. You can understand why the captains of these great tankers slow their speed right down when there are big waves so that they're not caught straddling several waves at once.

Dyna is an experimental petrol tanker with rigid, fold-away sails.

The dimensions of the giant tanker *Batillus:* 414 metres long, 62 metres wide, height of the hull 36 metres, laden weight 634,000 tonnes, unladen weight 75,000 tonnes, speed 16 knots.

The cabin boy

*. . . Then up stepped the little cabin boy,
And a pretty boy was he.
He says: 'Oh, I grieve for my own mother dear,
Whom I nevermore shall see.*

*Last night, when the moon shined bright,
My mother had sons five,
But now she may look in the salt salt seas
And find but one alive.'*

*Call a boat, call a boat, my fair Plymouth boys,
Don't you hear how the trumpets sound?
For the want of a long-boat in the ocean we were lost,
And most of our merry men drowned.*

A shanty

Fishermen

The sea is a source of great wealth: fish. At first, because fish does not stay fresh for long, it was eaten regularly only in regions near to the sea. Later, with the development of methods of salting and smoking, and then of freezing, it became possible to eat fish that had been caught some time before. People who lived far from the sea tasted seafood for the first time.

Throughout history men have fished the sea, some with lines and nets along the coast, while others leave hearth and home and the safety of the shore to go out deep sea fishing.

Fishing with nets

A fish on a line is all very fine, but there's something rather spectacular about fish leaping in nets.

Fishermen along the coast use a *seine* net (1). The net is rowed out in a small boat, and then dragged in by men waiting ashore. The fish are caught by the incoming net.

The big modern tuna boats also use seines when they're fishing in tropical waters.

Sardines and anchovies are caught in *trammel* nets (2). These are made up of three layers of net, with two large-meshed nets on the outside, and a very fine net in the middle. You can see a trammel net in the picture below, moored between two buoys. The bottom line is weighted with lead so that the net will hang down. After it has been in the sea several hours the

> *But up jumps the fisherman
> stalwart and grim
> And with his big net he scoops
> them all in.* Traditional song

fishermen will haul it in, and pull it, and whatever is caught in it, aboard their boat.

The *bag-net* (3) is a pocket-like net which the boat trails out behind it. It catches everything in its path. Some bag-nets are moored in tide-ways, and emptied at the turn of the tide. There is a very large one like this, called a stow-net, anchored off the east coast of England.

There are also bigger *trawl-nets* (4), which can be over 100 metres wide at the mouth. They operate at great depths, and almost always have to be trawled by two boats working together.

A *shrimping net* is pushed along the surface of the sand or seaweed to catch shrimps.

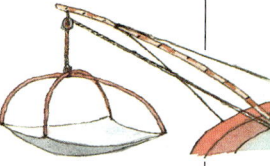

The *dip-net* is used for fishing for flat fish in shallow waters. It can be pulled up quickly if a bank or rock gets in the way.

'It was...

A specialized and very exciting form of fishing is bonito, or tunny fishing.

The French fish for bonito and its smaller cousin, the albacore, in the Bay of Biscay. They use, or rather used, for the boats are now becoming rare, sleek, fast sailing boats with distinctive beautiful brown sails. Six long fishing lines trailed out from two booms, one each side of the boat, with two other lines trailing from the stern. Each line had on it a double hook, usually hidden inside a bundle of straw or horsehair. As the boat raced through the water, the fish would rush at the hooks. They were quickly hauled on board and immediately cleaned and hung on a wooden frame amidships, ready to be sent to the canning factory.

The *hooker* is a long line trailed parallel to the sea bed. It may sometimes be miles long. Hanging from it are hundreds, even thousands, of shorter lines, each ending in a baited hook.

...*this* big.'

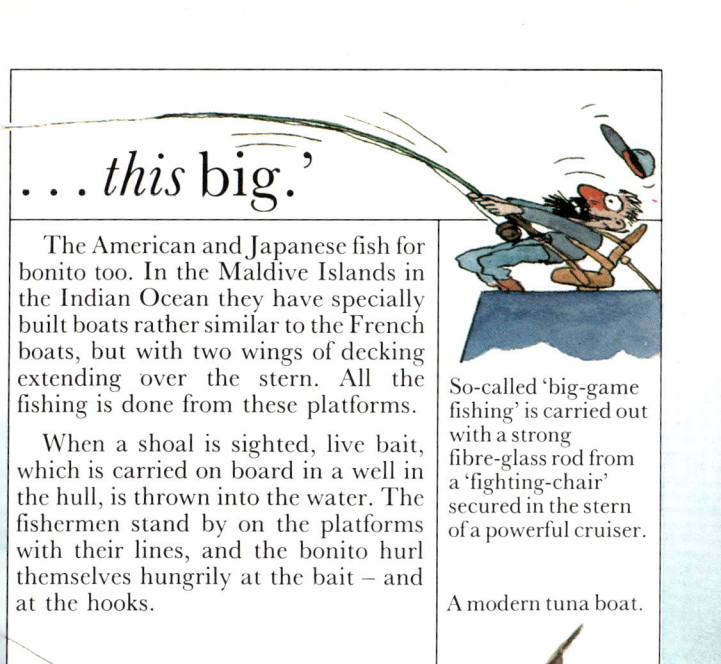

The American and Japanese fish for bonito too. In the Maldive Islands in the Indian Ocean they have specially built boats rather similar to the French boats, but with two wings of decking extending over the stern. All the fishing is done from these platforms.

When a shoal is sighted, live bait, which is carried on board in a well in the hull, is thrown into the water. The fishermen stand by on the platforms with their lines, and the bonito hurl themselves hungrily at the bait – and at the hooks.

So-called 'big-game fishing' is carried out with a strong fibre-glass rod from a 'fighting-chair' secured in the stern of a powerful cruiser.

A modern tuna boat.

Whaling

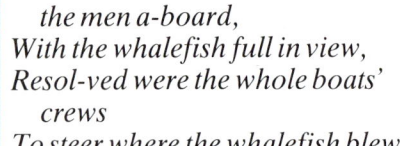

*Now the boats were launched and the men a-board,
With the whalefish full in view,
Resol-ved were the whole boats' crews
To steer where the whalefish blew, brave boys,
To steer where the whalefish blew.*

A whaling song

'Boats out!'

'Strike! Strike!'

''Ware the tail!'

'Our markers in.'

Two whales in tow: a good catch.

No sooner had men begun to explore the sea than they discovered these great 'sea-monsters'. Whales have been hunted since the earliest times, prized for their blubber, their bones and their meat. The blubber could be boiled down into oil, great vats of it (you can see the thick black smoke from the boiling blubber in the ship below), while a single whale could provide more meat than a hundred bullocks.

Specialized whaling boats were developed, carrying harpoons for spearing the whale and ropes for towing it back to the ship, where it could be flayed and cut up.

A whaler with its coiled harpoon rope.

The mother ship waits while the crew goes out in the whalers, risking the whale's lashing tail as they close in to throw their harpoons. Nowadays harpoons have exploding heads and are fired from the decks of big ships.

Harpoon

Pilots

The pilot waits on shore, ready to guide ships in difficult coastal waters: up rivers, through channels, into or out of port.

The pilot here is being taken out to the big ship in a sailing boat. When he gets close, he launches a dinghy and rows out to the ship. He has to climb aboard up a swinging rope ladder – not easy in rough weather. When he is safely aboard, his mates in the sailing boat pick up the dinghy and head back to port. The pilot will stay on the ship and steer her safely in.

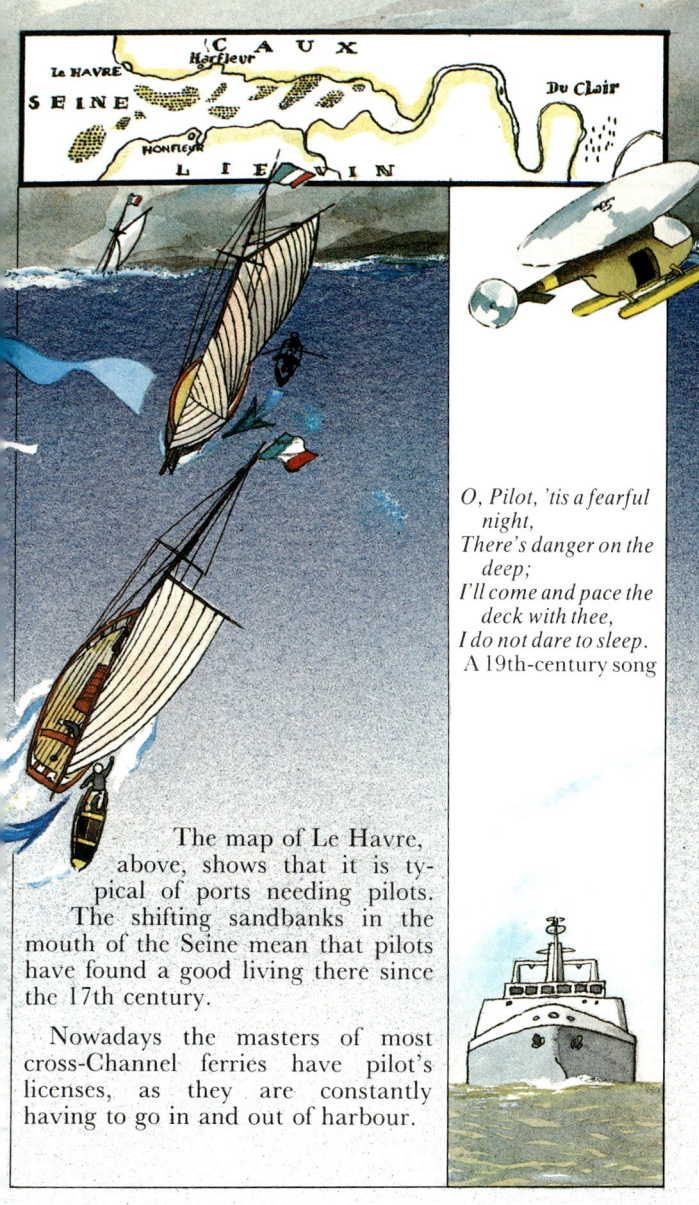

*O, Pilot, 'tis a fearful night,
There's danger on the deep;
I'll come and pace the deck with thee,
I do not dare to sleep.*
A 19th-century song

The map of Le Havre, above, shows that it is typical of ports needing pilots. The shifting sandbanks in the mouth of the Seine mean that pilots have found a good living there since the 17th century.

Nowadays the masters of most cross-Channel ferries have pilot's licenses, as they are constantly having to go in and out of harbour.

77

Lifeboats

Storms at sea mean ships in danger, and ships in danger mean lives at risk. Somehow there have always been brave men willing to set out to sea in the worst conditions, putting their own lives at risk to try and save their fellow seamen.

Once they simply rowed out in large rowing boats, pulling against the mountainous waves (you can see them in the picture below, heading for the desperate figures bobbing in the water).

Nowadays lifeboats (1) have radios and engines, and are designed to be self-righting if they capsize.

Many rescues which used to call for boats can now be carried out by helicopter. The occupant of the wrecked motor-boat opposite (2) is being winched up to safety at the end of a cable. A lifebelt (3) thrown to somebody in the water helps him to stay afloat.

Boats carry much more safety equipment than they used to: distress rockets, lifebelts, inflatable lifeboats, flares, radios.

Some inflatable lifeboats come ready packed (4). When thrown into the sea (5), they inflate automatically. Shipwrecked sailors can climb into the lifeboats and find shelter and emergency provisions ready for them. There they are safe from the cold and wet, while the flashing beacon and the radio homing signal (6) help rescuers to find them.

Under the sea

Until the 18th century exploration of the sea was confined to its surface. Even the bravest of divers could not overcome two inevitable problems: lack of air and, at any depth, pressure.

The painter and inventor Leonardo da Vinci thought about the problem and designed an aqualung. But it stayed on the drawing-board.

A few adventurous people tried diving with baskets full of air over their heads, or while sucking tubes attached to air-filled bladders, but neither method was very satisfactory.

Now that the two problems of air supply and pressure have been almost entirely solved, underwater exploration is a reality.

Jacques Cousteau, the famous French underwater explorer, uses his oceanographic ship *Calypso* (1) as a base, diving off it with aqualungs (2) and diving saucers (3), with an ever-increasing understanding of the world under the sea and of the techniques needed to explore it.

The inventor Auguste Piccard developed his bathyscaphe *Trieste* so as to be able to descend to depths beyond 11,000 metres and explore the strange dark world where daylight never penetrates and the creatures of the sea are luminous and nearly blind.

The main application of diving today, though, is more for construction than for exploration. Divers inspect underwater damage to shipping and can carry out minor repairs themselves.

The great platforms and pipelines that drill and carry oil from under the North Sea could never have been built without divers, in aqualungs, diving-suits, or, at greater depth, pressurized diving-bells of reinforced cast steel. Divers inspect and repair the oil-rigs constantly.

If divers have to work in docks and harbours they often have difficulty seeing what they are doing because of all the mud. Even though they have powerful torches, they still have to do a lot simply by touch.

Divers also help in salvaging sunken ships by fixing to them the great cables which are used to haul them to the surface.

Jacques Cousteau

Auguste Piccard . . .

and *Trieste*.

The last great sailing ships

The First World War (1914-18) hastened the end of the sailing ship. After the war, passengers and goods were transported on mechanically propelled ships.

The Russian ship *Krusenstern*, which belongs to the Soviet Navy.

The English use the sailing ship *Winston Churchill* as a training-ship for naval cadets.

By good fortune, though, a few voluntary associations and some navies have seen fit to preserve some rare survivors from the golden age of sail.

There can be few more exciting sights than to see several such ships gathered together, and to watch the grace of these 'canvas cathedrals'.

1. The *Reliance*, winner in 1903.
2. The *Ranger*, winner in 1937.
3. A 12m JI of the 1950s.

The America's Cup

In 1851, five rich Americans sent their brand new schooner to race against the English. Their boat left all the English yachts standing and won a cup which came to be called the *America's Cup*. For over 100 years the English, and then the Canadians, the Australians, the French, the Swedes and the Italians tried to take the cup away from the Americans. A hundred years during which the schooners and great sail-clad cutters gave way to the smaller 12 metre JI-class boats. A hundred years during which captains of industry and finance battled it out against each other paying for ever-faster ships. Until the day when ... on **26 September 1983,** the 12m *Australia II* beat the American ship *Liberty*. The cup had finally changed hands.

Index

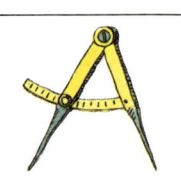

Actium 11
Africa 45
Alecto 62
Alexander
  the Great 11
Alfred the Great 11
America 24, 27,
  30-31, 34-5, 45, 57
America's Cup,
  the 14-15, 84-5
Amundsen,
  Roald 58
Anthony 11
Aotooroo 47
Arabs, the 11
arbaletus 52
Archduke Ludovic 62
Archimedes
  screw 62
Ariel 57
Armada 13, 32-3
astrolabe 52
astronomy 20-21
Athens 22

Atlantic Ocean 11, 19, 28, 64
Named after the mythical Greek figure Atlas, who carried the world on his shoulders. The Atlas mountains stand at the Western end of the Mediterranean.

Attila the Hun 11
Augustus,
  Emperor 11
Australia 13, 46, 57
Australia II 15
Aztecs 31

Babylon 10
Bahamas, the 37
Balbao, Vasco
  Nuñes de 28, 31
Barents, William 58
Batillus 67
bireme 22
Blackbeard (Edward
  Teech) 38-9
Boston 35
Bougainville, Comte
  de 13, 46-7
Bounty, mutiny
  on 14, 50-51
Britain, Great 24

Cadiz 20, 55
Calais 33
canoes 10
Castor 62
Champlain,
  Samuel de 13
Charles I, King
  of England 13
clippers 56-7
Coleridge, Samuel,
  *The Rime of the
  Ancient Mariner* 14
Columbus, Christo-
  pher 12, 26-8
Commerson,
  Philibert 48
compass, the 12, 61
Conde de Tolosa 36
Condent, Jack 39
container ships 66
Cook, James 13, 46,
  48-9, 51
corsairs 38-9
Cortés, Her-
  nando 12, 30-31
corvus 23
Cousteau,
  Jacques 15, 80
Crete 10

Davis quadrant 52
Defoe, Daniel,
  Robinson Crusoe 13
dhows 60-61
Discovery 59
Drake, Francis 32
Dyna 67

Easter Island 46
Egypt 10
Egyptians 10, 19, 53
Elise 14
Elizabeth I, Queen
  of England 13
Endurance 15, 59
England 25
Eric the Red 11, 25

fishing 69-73
Fram 15, 58-9
France 20, 24

galleons 33, 36-7
galleys 13, 22, 42-3
Gama, Vasco da 12
Gibraltar,
  Straits of 19
Great Eastern 14
Designed to travel non-stop to Australia, she had both paddle-wheels and a screw, five funnels and six masts.

Greece 22
Greenland 11, 24

Henry the
  Navigator 12
Henry VIII, King of
  England 12, 41
Herodotus 11, 19
Heyerdahl, Thor 19
Hovercraft, the 63

Indian Ocean 19
Ionian Sea 11
Ireland 33
Isabella, Queen
  of Spain 26-7

James I, King
  of England 13
Japan 26
JI-class boats 84-5
junks 60-61

Kidd, Captain 38
knots 53
An essential part of a sailor's life.

Liberty 15
lifeboats 78-9

Lifeboats and other life-saving equipment on boats first became a statutory requirement in England in 1894.

87

liners	64-5	
log-line	53	
longships	25	

Macedonia 11
Magellan, Ferdinand 12, 28-9
Mahomet 11
Manhattan 34
Marco Polo 12
Mary Rose 40-41
Mayflower 13, 34-5

Mediterranean Sea 10-11, 19-20
Mediterranean means 'middle of the earth' in Latin. It was the centre of the known world to the Greeks and Romans.

Melville, Herman, *Moby Dick* 15
Mexico 30-31
Montezuma 31
Morgan, Henry 13
Moses 10

Nansen, Fridtjof 15, 58-9
Nautilus 15
navigation 52-3
Nelson, Horatio 54-5
Nina 27
nocturnal 52
Normandie 63, 65
North Pole 15, 58-9

octant 52
By using a reflecting mirror, it doubled the degree of altitude which could be measured by the common quadrant.

Pacific Ocean 12, 28-9, 48
Parkinson, Sidney 48
Peary, Robert Edwin 15, 58
Philip II, King of Spain 13, 32-3
Phoenicians 10, 19, 53
Piccard, Auguste 15, 81
Pilgrim Fathers 34-4
pilots 76-7

Pinta 27
pirates 38-9
Pizarro, Francisco 31
Polynesia 10, 46
Portugal 20, 28
Pytheas 11, 20-21

quadrant 52
Quadrants and octants measured the height of the stars,

Queen Elizabeth II 63, 65

Rā 19
Rackam, 'Calico Jack' 39
Ranger 84
Rattler 62
Reliance 84
Roberts, Bartholomew 39

Salamis, battle of 11, 22	*Thomas Anderson* 63	*Wasa* 40-41
sampans 61	Themistocles 22	West Indies, the 27, 45
San Salvador 27	Thule 21	whaling 74-5
Santa Maria 27	*Titanic* 65	*Willapa* 62
Savannah 63	Trafalgar 54-5	William the Conqueror 11
Scotland 33	traverse-board 52	*Winston Churchill* 83
Scott, Robert Falcon 15, 58-9	*Trieste* 15, 81	
Selkirk, Alexander 13	Troy 10	

Serica 57

Shackleton, Ernest Henry 15
After his ship broke up in the ice in 1914, he led his party in open boats to safety at Elephant Island. Leaving them in camp, he and five others sailed a further 800 miles for help.

Ulysses 10, 16-17
As well as the Sirens, Ulysses met a one-eyed giant, Polyphemus, who ate shipwrecked sailors.

Sinbad the Sailor 17
slavery 14, 42-5
South Pole 15, 58-9
Spain 20, 28-9, 33
Stevenson, Robert Louis, *Treasure Island* 15
Stockholm 40
Surcouf, Robert 38

Verrazzano, Giovanni da 34
Victoria 29
Victoria, Queen of England 15
Vikings, the 24-5
Villeneuve, Pierre Charles de 55

Xerxes, King of the Persians 22

Yacht
From the Dutch word *jacht* meaning pleasure-boat.

Taeping 57
Tahiti 47, 51
tankers, petrol 66-7

Zenith
The highest point of observation for navigation.

89

Biographies

Dominique Duviard was born in Nantes, in France, in 1940. From early boyhood, he loved sailing around the coasts of Brittany. Working as an ecologist and tropical biologist, he spent 10 years in Africa. On his return to France, he wrote books about the history of fishing and sailing, and spent all his free time sailing with his wife and children. Sadly, he died of a heart condition in 1984.

Tony Ross has been one of the leading children's book illustrators in England since the publication of his first picture book in 1973. A great number of his 50 picture books, including the popular *Towser* series, have been published in many different countries. He teaches art, and is senior lecturer at Manchester Art School. Less well-known is his long-standing fascination with marine painting, and his own abilities as a marine painter. As a penniless young artist, he would paint for himself the pictures of the sea and ships that he could not afford to buy.

In the 'Discoverers' series, Tony Ross has also illustrated *Painting and Painters*.

Acknowledgements

The editor and publisher wish to thank the following for permission to use copyright material:

Jonathan Cape Ltd for the extract from *The Child and the Mariner* by W.H. Davies; The Estate of Rudyard Kipling for the extract from *The Song of the Galley Slaves* by Rudyard Kipling; William Heinemann Ltd and Macmillan Co, N.Y. for the extract from *Cargoes* by John Masefield.

Every effort has been made to trace copyright but if any omissions have been made please let us know in order that we may put it right in the next edition.

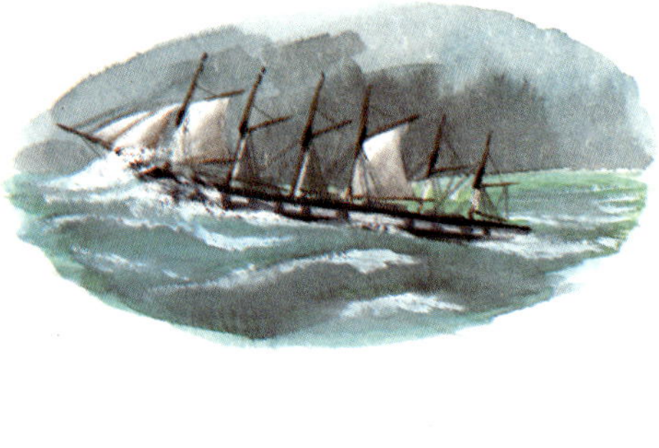